Help! I'm a New Team Leader

Help! I'm a New Team Leader

Coaching for the Leader of the Team

Robert O. Noah

Writers Club Press
San Jose New York Lincoln Shanghai

Help! I'm a New Team Leader
Coaching for the Leader of the Team

Writers Club Press
an imprint of iUniverse.com, Inc.

For information address:
iUniverse.com, Inc.
620 North 48th Street, Suite 201
Lincoln, NE 68504-3467
www.iuniverse.com

ISBN: 0-595-13374-6

Printed in the United States of America

To my students and my teachers.

Contents

Chapter I

The New Challenge of Leadership

It was a hot, muggy day when Maury arrived at the plant to start his new job as team leader. He wasn't new at Hutching Incorporated. He had actually worked there more than eight years. But the team leader position was new for him. He had started there the summer he graduated from high-school. It was a part time job disassembling defective units for recycling. Over the years he learned the skills on the front lines and took on increased responsibility when he had the opportunity.

He understood how things worked and what it took to get things done around Hutching.

Maury had known his share of bosses, both kinds, the bad and the ugly. He actually had some good ones, too. Often he wished he could be in their shoes. Now he had landed his first leadership position. He felt a little heady.

As he walked in, he could see the men and women who had been his peers watching. They were all smiles and hand shakes. It was a good feeling.

He was scheduled for team leader orientation though he didn't really think he needed it. After all, he had years of experience and a record of accomplishment that made him stand out from his peers. Never-the-less, he thanked his friends who had stepped forward to congratulate him, turned down the hall and went into the training room as he had been instructed.

A folder was laid out with the team leader job description and a note pad. Jody, his supervisor followed him in. She had recommended Maury for the position and had helped him out by giving him extra cross training so he knew more about the whole operation. So she was assigned to orient him.

She asked, "Have you read the job description?"

He had, and said, "Sure."

"Do you have any questions?" She continued.

He couldn't think of any. "No, not really."

She described the lines of authority and told him the expected level of production. The orientation was over. "Well, I guess that's about it. Come on with me to the meeting room for the morning team leader meeting."

Maury followed her into the part of the office he had previously seen as an outsider. As he entered, he saw another group of familiar faces around the table. A couple of them were new to the position like him. Most were old hands in team leadership. They welcomed him as he came in.

Mark, the plant manager, spoke, "Welcome and congratulations. Let's get started right away." He shook Maury's hand, waved him to a seat and addressed the group, "Maury, whom you all know, is now the team leader in shipping and receiving." He introduced the other new team leaders, one who came from outside the company, and went on to make announcements concerning the work for the day.

Maury took the printouts that were handed out. They told what would be coming and what had gone out the previous day. The papers were like the ones he had seen posted every day since he had started working, but now there was a difference. He had the responsibility of making sure the deadlines and quotas were met.

The meeting was over quickly and everyone went out to do their job. But what was his job? He knew how to do each of the tasks out in the shipping and receiving department and knew there were enough people to do them all on this day. He just didn't know what his job was.

As he got to the desk, he was met by Mark. "Maury, today is the first day. Do you have any questions?"

Maury felt a little like the new kid in kindergarten, "I can't think of any."

"Well, you know where to find me if you need me," Mark said with an expression that suggested he expected to hear from Maury pretty soon.

Maury started to look over the stuff on his desk to see if he needed anything when he saw a shadow out of the corner of his eye. He looked up and saw a young man with red hair down over his collar, bulging Adam's apple and plaid shirt, one of the new guys. "Can I help you?" Maury asked.

"Well, I was just wondering if I should..." He was asking a question about a common procedure, one for which he should know the answer.

Maury listened patiently and answered the question by giving the same instructions which had been given to them all several days before when the procedure was initiated. The redheaded guy thanked him, said, "I just wanted to be sure that's the way you wanted it done," and went out to work. Maury felt something strange.

As the plaid shirted employee walked away, Maury felt like his neck was on the line. His success or failure was in the hands of that new kid. It didn't feel all that comfortable. It was like that guy had managed to get Maury's fingerprints on his murder weapon. If things didn't work out, the kid would be off the hook. It would be Maury's fault. If they did, the red-haired guy could chalk it up as a personal success, no responsibility and no risk.

About that time he looked out at the line and saw the work team standing around not doing a thing. Maury went out and asked what was wrong.

"Keep your shirt on." Linda was speaking for the group. She had worked alongside him until today and she had always kind of pushed things to the limit. It had been amusing when he wasn't the team leader. Now it wasn't.

She said, "There's no rush. It takes a while for things to get started up. You know that. Besides, we're no farther behind than we were yesterday. And by the time the shift is over we will be about as far behind as we are today."

"Come on folks," he joked, "let's get to work." He had another shot of the same feeling he had earlier. Another load of responsibility was transferred from their shoulders to his.

He pitched in, working side by side with them, not like other team leaders he had known down through the years who just stood around and watched. He was trying to set a good example, trying to get ahead, trying to get his numbers to look a little better than they had before he was the team leader.

By the end of the day he was beat. He had worked hard all day, answered a lot of questions which he thought his people should know the answers to, ran from place to place making sure the work got done, and jumped in to rescue the doubtful.

He earned his pay. But when he looked again at the printout he had posted at the start of the shift, he saw that he was even farther behind than yesterday. They were even farther behind schedule then they had been when he started.

As Maury left to go home, he passed Mark's office. Mark was busy on the phone. Maury didn't want to appear weak but wondered how he was going to succeed in improving his department when he couldn't get a normal day's work done even when he pulled out all the stops.

How was he ever going to get ahead? And how would he know if he was making any headway. He didn't even know which way to go.

He thought, "Thank God it's Friday. Maybe things will go better on Monday."

Chapter II

Take Charge of Your Life

Saturday morning found Maury at the hardware store picking up some plumbing stuff for his new bathroom project in his basement. As he compared fixture prices and styles he heard someone speak his name.

"Maury, isn't it?" The voice came from behind him. As he turned, he saw his neighbor, a man with blond hair streaked with silver, about the age of Maury's father, dressed in a sweater and pushing a cart containing a single roll of grey duct tape.

"Oh. Hi, Noah." Maury had a passing acquaintance with his neighbor but had never really gotten to know him. He remembered Noah telling him once that he was involved in developing people. Maury didn't really know what that meant and hadn't asked either.

"Heard you got a promotion," Noah smiled.

"Yeah, I am a team leader now," Maury responded.

"What a coincidence, Maury," Noah remarked. "I'm a coach.".

Maury laughed, "It's not that kind of team. We're not starting up a baseball team. I am a new leader of a work team."

Noah smiled, "It's a good thing. I don't know that much about baseball. But I have a little experience with teamwork at work, So, how is it going with your team?"

"I don't know exactly. " Maury answered. "I just got started yesterday and I'm not sure I really know what I should be doing. I thought I could make a difference and thought the team would respect me if I jumped in and worked beside them. But after the day was through, I wasn't sure what I did made any difference at all."

Maury went on to explain the feeling that he had taken on more responsibility than he had expected and the frustration of starting behind and not getting anywhere.

> *"A leader must be able to see the end results of the policies and methods he or she advocates. Responsible leadership always looks ahead to see how policies will affect future generations."*
>
> —*J. Oswald Sanders*[1]

"Are you interested in finding the answers to those problems or are you just complaining?" Noah replied sounding genuinely concerned.

"Actually I was just griping. But if there really is a solution I'm interested," Maury said, not really expecting his neighbor to know how to solve his problem. He had thought he would just have to work it out as he went along. But now that the idea was planted in his mind he wondered if Noah knew something that could help him out.

Noah looked at his watch. "I have some time this afternoon if you'd like to stop by."

Maury did a quick estimate of the work he had to do on his basement plumbing project and responded, "I think I'd like to."

Noah said, "Before you come over, I have an assignment for you to complete."

"Okay," laughed Maury, "what do you want me to do?"

"Do you have a paper and pencil?" Noah watched Maury fumble in his shirt pocket. "I see that you do. Write down this question. 'Which drives which, process or result?' When you come over, I want you to tell me the answer."

Maury wrote the question on the back of his shopping list. When he looked up, Noah had already headed down the isle. "I'll see you this afternoon," he called after his disappearing neighbor.

---

[1] J. Oswald Sanders, *Spiritual Leadership*, Moody Press, Chicago (1994).

When he got home, he lugged the result of his morning's shopping spree down to the basement. He took out the shopping list and read the question he had written on the back. He thumb tacked it up on the board he was using to keep track of his bathroom project.

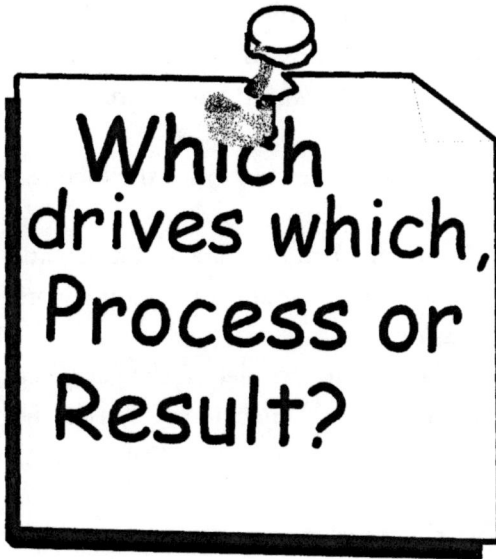

The answer seemed simple enough. It was perfectly obvious that every process has a result. The process drives the result. Right? Of course, right. He decided he would tell Noah that process drives result.

Maury began to look through his plumbing supplies. As he laid them out, he looked up on the board. He had a diagram of his 'perfect bathroom' all drawn with dimensions and a list of materials he would need including the finishing touch, an antique bathtub with legs.

He began to check off the items he had picked up at the store when he saw the question posted there beside his bathroom plans. It is true that picking up the parts was part of the process that would produce the bathroom of his dreams but there on the board he had the evidence that he had already determined what the result would be before the process was ever started.

> *"Your Words do not just*
> *represent your reality,*
> *they help to shape it."*[2]

He started putting the parts together. He hadn't worked very long before he discovered he had missed something. His picture was not detailed enough and he knew he would have to make another trip to town before he could go on.

Maury drew in the detail he needed to see the picture better and wrote down a few more items on the list.

After lunch, Maury took a pad of paper and a pen and walked over to Noah's house. He decided that if Noah had anything worthwhile to say, he wanted to be sure to get it down.

He could hear and see Noah occupied in the garage cutting some aged oak branches on his scroll saw. When Noah paused, Maury cleared his throat and startled Noah. "Oh hi, Maury," Noah said. "Come on in."

Maury pulled up a stool at Noah's invitation and got out his pen and pad. "I'm ready, Coach. I hope you can help me out. I may have bitten off more than I can chew."

Noah was holding a short length of an oak branch in his hand as he asked, "Tell me Maury, which drives which, process or result?" As Noah spoke, he poked the end of the branch into the air in two places to indicate the two options.

Maury was ready for his question. "When I first thought about it, I was ready to say that process drives result because every process produces a result. But after considering the question for a while I decided the desired result must be determined before the process can be designed.

"So the result you want determines the process you design." With a tone of decision he said, "Result drives process."

---

[2] John Stewart, *Together: Interpersonal Communication*, Addison-Wesley (1980).

Noah looked at Maury like he was looking right through him and asked, "Maury, have you decided what result you want from your leadership position?"

The question hit Maury right between the eyes. He said, "I haven't even thought about it."

Noah continued, "Then it's no wonder you don't feel successful. You haven't defined success."

Maury felt a little foolish. He wondered how something so basic had escaped him. Still, he had a goal, to do better than they had done the day before. He wanted to catch up on back orders and send out shipments on time. That was a result that could be written down and measured.

Noah was still talking. "Maury, have you decided what result you want? Not just today or tomorrow, but what do you really want in the long run?"

"No. I don't even know where to start." Maury shook his head.

"Fortunately, I do." Said Noah. "We need to do a little time traveling. I have found that when you want to determine the result you should always start in the future."

Chapter III

Core Values

Time travel? Maury was lost. He wondered what this guy was talking about.

"Come with me on a journey to the other end of your life," said Noah.

"Why not?" sighed Maury. This made no sense at all. He wondered if there was a way to politely get out of there and go back to working in his basement. Never-the-less, he decided to humor Noah. What a nut case.

"This is a journey in your imagination." Noah was gesturing to the much-relieved Maury. It was starting to sound not quite so goofy. "The day we will picture is your retirement party. You are healthy, happy and have reached all your goals. This is a testimonial celebration of your life's accomplishments."

Maury was trying to picture this all in his mind as Noah described it.

"You have invited guests from every role of your life and each person gets to make a speech about you. And since this is your imagination, you get to decide what they will say."

Maury thought through the roles of his life. He was a team leader, father, husband, Little League coach, and home fix-it man.

Noah took out an erasable marker and wrote on the side of an old refrigerator in his garage the word, 'Roles.' Maury told him the roles and Noah wrote them in a vertical column on the left side of the white space.

Next, Noah labeled a middle column, 'Representatives.' "Who would you like to invite to speak? Pick someone who represents each of the roles."

Maury took the marker and wrote 'Red' next to 'team leader.' Red was the new kid he had helped yesterday. Below that he wrote 'Heidi,' 'Peg,' 'Danny,' and 'Bob Vila' next to the roles listed on the left side.

Noah said, "Okay, now put one more role down, your essential person. And in the center column, list a hero of yours."

Maury blushed a little, then wrote 'personal' at the bottom of the left column and 'Abraham Lincoln' in the center column. "He's always been a hero of mine since I read about him in school."

Roles	**Representatives**	**Values**

Noah led the way again. "Now it is time for each of these guests to speak. You get to decide what they will say. Let's start at the top. You have listed 'Red' under that column. Imagine he is standing to speak to the crowd. What do you want him to say about you?"

Noah wrote 'Values' at the top of a third column on the right side of the make shift white board.

Maury decided to play along. "Well, Red is one of my people, but by that time he will be an old man. I want him to say, 'One thing I appreciate about Maury is that he helped me grow as an employee.'"

Noah wrote "helped me grow" to the right of Red's name.

"And I want him to say, 'Maury was fair and made the job enjoyable.'" added Maury.

Noah added 'fair' and 'made work enjoyable' to the list beside Red's name.

Maury was getting the hang of this. He went down through the role representatives describing their speeches. Soon the old refrigerator's side held a list of characteristics which Maury would like to have ascribed to him when he has accomplished everything he wants to accomplish in his life. It included 'fun,' 'sees the big picture,' 'dependability,' 'willing to take a chance' and several others. Some were repeated beside several roles.

Finally he got to his hero, Abraham Lincoln. "I want him to say, 'Maury dreamed big dreams and was willing to pay the price to reach them.'" Noah added those qualities to the list of values written on the side of the refrigerator.

Maury stepped back and looked at the list. It really described his inner drives.

Noah said, "These are your values. Look among them and see which characteristics apply to several of the roles." He handed Maury the marker.

Maury circled several which were listed more than once including 'fair,' 'fun,' 'big picture,' and 'willing to pay the price.'

"The ones you circled are your core driving values." Noah pointed from one to another of the circled words. "Do you think they describe what makes you tick?"

Maury nodded, "They really do. I don't think I have ever seen my values laid out so clearly."

Noah continued, "The core values you hold are seeds that will grow your future. But they won't do any good if they're not connected to your everyday life. What would you say are some of your life goals, some significant accomplishments which would support your core driving values?"

Maury sat back down and thought about it. After a while he said, "Well, there is the one I have just achieved, becoming a team leader."

Noah was obviously listening and paying attention but didn't say anything.

Seeds That Grow Your Future

"I want to see my daughter graduate from college," Maury continued. Before long he had life goals that matched each of the roles he had identified earlier.

"Now," Noah spoke earnestly as he gestured with both hands cupped together, "with what activities must you fill your days to reach those life goals."

This took more time but Noah was patient.

Eventually Maury had a list which he wrote on his pad. It included taking time to coach Red and all the other 'Reds' whose lives he wanted to help grow. Planning time, family activities, personal reflection and recreation all were listed by the time he was done.

When he had finished, he shared the activities with Noah. Noah said, "When you wake up in the morning, do you ever have a feeling of 'morning reluctance?' You know, the feeling that you wish you didn't have to go to work today? It is a sign that the activities you are anticipating may be in conflict with your core values. It is a signal to take stock of your activities and see if they are in line with your goals and values.

"Recognizing the connection between daily activities, goals and values can help you keep your courage and endurance when you are tempted to give up. It can help you pick among alternatives and find the ones that will pay off for you."

Then Noah said, "Now you can take this lesson home with you. Before you go to work on Monday think about what you want from your new position. Line up your goals with your core driving values. Then you can list activities you want to include which will help you achieve success."

"Noah, would you be willing to coach me along on this?" asked Maury.

Noah said, "Sure. Why don't we get together next Saturday at the same time?"

"That would be great." said Maury.

Chapter IV

Responsibilities of Leadership

Maury was encouraged. He could hardly wait to go back to work on Monday and was turning to go.

"I have another assignment for you," said Noah.

Maury turned back toward Noah while Noah continued, "As you go through your work days, keep track of the kind of power you use with your team."

"I'm not sure what you mean." Maury looked puzzled.

"There are two kinds of power. Position power and person power," said Noah.

"Position power is legitimate power and comes from the title you hold. It is the authority given to you by people higher than you.

"Personal power, on the other hand, is more who you are than what you are. It is your ability to influence people personally, to inspire, encourage, challenge, and make a difference from an inner source.

Position power can be given and taken away but personal power goes with you wherever you go."

Maury wrote the assignment down on his pad.

Maury got to Hutching early on Monday, hoping Mark would be there. He was, and Maury knocked at the edge of the office doorway. Mark looked up, smiled and nodded him in. "Mark, I want to be successful at my new job and at the end of my first day I didn't feel very successful."

"I saw your numbers." Mark said with a half smile that said he had half expected that result. "I was hoping you could get them up a bit, but it was your first day. I'm sure you'll get the hang of it."

That wasn't enough for Maury. "Maybe you could help me out a little." He paused, then said, "What would you say is the real job of the team leader?" He was fishing for the definition of result that would help him design the process for success.

"The real job of a team leader is to support the workforce." said Mark.

"Okay?" questioned Maury. It seemed perfectly obvious but he hadn't thought of it that way before.

"There are four responsibilities that define how that is done: plan, organize, coach and control." Mark made four imaginary piles on the front of his desk to represent the responsibilities. "That is how you accomplish the real job of a team leader."

Maury thought about that as he headed into the meeting room for the day's assignments. After listening to the others report on their departments, Maury took his turn. He stated plainly the goal figures and the insufficient actual figures.

No one looked surprised or even seemed to notice that there was a wide gap between the goal and the actual numbers. He wasn't really out of line with what the others were doing.

He could see that it would be possible to just get comfortable lagging behind the goals like the rest. But, remembering his session in Noah's garage, he knew that wasn't in line with his values. Something more was needed.

Maury started keeping track of his use of the different kinds of power. At the same time he kept in mind the definition Mark had given him, support the workforce, along with the list of activities that would accomplish the job: plan, organize, coach, and control. It wasn't difficult at all. He just kept a diary of his actions and in the margin beside each one he wrote the appropriate power category and leadership responsibility.

As he entered his work area, he looked over the printout and the list of expectations. He thought about how to best attack the work for the day before he went onto the floor to meet his team. He could see that was part of the 'plan' part of the job. He wrote the first item on his list, "Decide how to get today's work done."

Looking back at his list of criteria, he wrote 'plan' under that. Looking again he saw that it fit within his concept of himself as a leader. Anyone could make time to make plans. It was not the kind of activity that was tied to his position. This was personal leadership, the kind of thinking that had helped him get promoted to this position of team leader in the first place.

Maury took his note pad with him as he went out to assign the work tasks. "Linda, the first line is going to be loaded constantly with more products than usual. I want you to make sure that line is covered. If you get behind, let me know right away so we can bring someone in to keep it up."

Maury explained the extra sense of urgency regarding the product on that line. Linda went right to it while Maury turned to another of his people. "John, your line will be a little lighter than Linda's." John was a steady but quiet worker who had been with the company since the expansion the previous fall. He continued speaking with John, "She will tell you if she needs your help." Maury continued down the line, letting each person know the place he or she would fill in his grand plan.

He stepped to a table and opened up his pad. The assignment of tasks fit the category of organizing. He wrote it there. Thinking about the power bases, he penciled in 'position power'. "This may take some personal power," he thought, "but the primary reason the people are doing what I say is because I have the position of team leader."

As he was writing, John signaled him to come over to the line.

"What do you need?" Maury asked when he arrived at John's side.

"Can I ask you something?" John asked.

"Sure." Maury responded.

"Well, I just wanted to know…" John was asking about scheduling a vacation day in the next week.

As John was speaking, Maury saw that John's handling technique was taking much more effort than was needed. Maury used to do this very job and knew some tricks.

"No problem," Maury said, referring to the vacation request, then continued after a slight pause. "John, watch how I do this." Maury stepped to the line and used his years of practiced skill to handle the item John had been struggling with. "If you do it like this it takes much less effort and you actually get it done faster." Maury was demonstrating as he explained." John said he would try it next time and Maury left him to his work.

Maury opened his pad again and wrote two more activities. The first was giving permission to take the vacation day. The second was showing John a better technique for product handling. Under the 'permission' item he wrote, "control," thinking that there might have been a better time and way of handling that one. But it was an activity that fit into the controlling responsibility of a team leader.

Beside 'control' he wrote "position power." The only reason he could give John the day off was because of his position. Under the item related to showing John how to do his job better, he wrote, "coach." Next to that he listed, "personal power." It knew that he was using the same kind of leadership skill that he had been using before he was the team leader.

He kept a list of these activities, categorizing each one as best he could under the four activities of a team leader; plan, organize, coach and control, as well as under the headings of legitimate power and personal power.

Throughout the week his list grew to fill several pages.

On Saturday he was in his basement again. He wasn't quite as far behind at work as he was the first day, but still not up to the level he wanted to achieve.

He opened his tool box to work on his bathroom project and said under his breath, "The right tool makes all the difference." He remembered those words from his father.

He heard a knock at the back door. He called out, "Come on in. I'm in the basement."

Noah's voice called out, "Maury?"

"Yeah, come on down." Maury heard Noah's feet on the stairs.

"Maury, I'm sorry to intrude on your project like this," said Noah.

"No," Maury set his tools aside and gave Noah his attention. "I've got plenty of time."

"Well, that's just it." Noah said. "I'm not going to be around this afternoon, but do I have some time this morning."

"How about right now?" said Maury. He could easily put his construction project off until later.

"I was hoping you would say that. It would make it a lot easier." Noah looked relieved.

Maury gestured toward a chair and took a seat on the second step of his step ladder. "Where do we start?"

"Did you do your homework?" Noah asked.

"Sure." Maury motioned for Noah to stay where he was, dashed up the stairs and returned in a moment with his notes. Between breaths he said, "I kept a list of the things I did under these categories." Maury explained Mark's definition of the team leader position and the four responsibilities.

Noah took the lists and looked them over. Spreading them out on the counter he said, "Do you see any relationships between the two kinds of lists?"

Maury looked them over. He noticed that some of the items he had listed under the four responsibilities were also listed under the two power categories. "It looks like the planning is related more to using personal power and organization is more related to position power."

Noah smiled.

Maury continued, "And the coaching is associated with personal power while the controlling is more closely related to position power." Maury watched Noah's approval and felt like he had gotten another piece of the puzzle into place.

Noah took a small piece of drywall trimming and knelt on the floor. He used it like a stick of chalk and drew a square divided into four squares. He wrote 'plan' in the upper left square, 'organize' in the lower left, 'coach' in the upper right, and 'control' in the lower right.

Then he made a diagonal mark from the upper right corner to the lower left corner. "You will notice," here Noah swept his hand in the air over his drawing, "that the more you can do those activities that fit in the upper left half, the less you have to do the activities that fit into the lower right half."

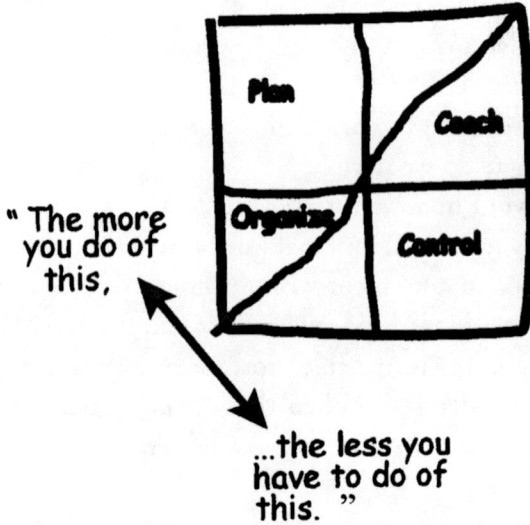

He looked Maury in the eye, "You have to do the activities that fit into all four categories, but your success and growth as a leader will depend on your ability to shift the weight of your activities to the upper left.

"When you find yourself struggling with organizing, look to see if your planning was adequate. When you are resorting to control tactics, look at the coaching options. When coaching and controlling start to take up too much of your time and energy, look to see if you could be doing more planning and organizing.

"Have you noticed that long handled tools give you better leverage?"

Maury nodded, "Sure. You don't have to put so much muscle into the work."

Noah explained, "The long handled tools of leadership make leading easier. It takes less personal pressure, less wrestling and less sweating."

Maury looked around at his bathroom project. "The right tool," he said to himself, "makes all the difference."

Noah said, "I'm going to have to go."

Maury nodded, deep in thought.

As Noah turned, Maury grabbed his sleeve, "Don't you have some homework for me?"

"Yes I do," said Noah.

Chapter V

Goal Setting

Noah smiled, "As a time traveler I have found it worthwhile to make some present moment investments that have a future payoff."

Maury was sure this was leading somewhere but he didn't know where. Noah continued, "It's time to start taking some action that will pay off in the future. One way to do that is to set some goals."

"I've already been thinking about that," said Maury. "I want to get my productivity higher, increase the skills of my team and in general do a better job."

Noah looked puzzled, "How will you know when you reach your goals, Maury?"

"Well, I don't know how I will know, but I'm sure I'll know it when I get there." Maury's voice sounded less sure than his words boasted.

"Maury, look around you here. Your bathroom project is nowhere near done." Noah was looking at Maury's plans posted on the board, the bare studs, the markings on the floor and piles of building materials.

"That's true, but look here at the brochure. This is what it will look like when I am done." Maury showed Noah the picture.

"If you have the picture on the front of the brochure, what do you need all that stuff for?" Noah pointed to the lists of needed parts, the ones with items checked off and the drawings for the various stages of the project.

"I think I know what you mean," Maury said. "I need to get a more detailed picture of what the final result will be in order to know when I get there."

Noah nodded, "There are eight rules that will help you."

Maury picked up his tablet and pencil.

Noah went on, "Rule number one, 'Goals must be written.' Written goals are able to be reviewed on a regular basis. Writing also generates a greater commitment to do what it takes to have the goals materialize." Noah wrote the rule on the lower half of a sheet of paper, folded it and hung it on the first rung of the step ladder.

"Rule number two," said Noah, "'Goals must be specific and measurable.' If the goal is general, such as 'reduce expense' or 'work harder,' it can not be measured. If you cannot measure the goal, you won't know if the goal has been accomplished."

Maury took over the task of writing the rules and hanging them on the rungs.

He could see that he had been much too general when he started talking about his goals. He would have to decide how to measure the productivity and his employees' work skills. For the productivity goal he decided that he would use the printout that the company handed out every day as the specific measurable goal.

Noah went on, "The third rule is, 'Goals must have a time deadline for attainment.' Many people never accomplish their goals because they think, 'Someday I'll get to it.' Put a time deadline on everything to be done. It creates a sense of urgency to accomplish the goal by that time."

Maury wrote, "Deadline." The deadline was a little harder to come up with. "Noah, this goal is a continuing goal. There isn't really a specific date."

"A lot of people tell me that," said Noah. "But as a seasoned time traveler, I have found that every goal has time dimensions. Think about it and see if there is a way to set the goal into a time frame." He waited for Maury to consider the time concern.

"I don't think I will be able to just start meeting the posted goal every day starting next Monday." His voice gave away his deep thinking process. "I don't want to take too long to be doing that either. I think I will set a target date to be achieving the assigned goal four out of five days by the end of two months."

"That brings us to the fourth one," Noah said. "Goals must be realistic and attainable." Noah's eyes were lifted as if he was remembering his list. Again they focused on Maury. "If the goal is unrealistic, the internal motivation to go after it disappears. On the other hand, the goal must be set high enough to provide a challenge, something beyond what has already been done."

Maury thought again of the daily goals which were passed out in the team leader meeting at work. It had been a long time since anyone had reached the goal which was posted. In fact, his team had started calling it the 'dream list.' Maury wrote, "Attainable but challenging."

"If leaders establish clear goals, it not only helps keep their organizations focused on what they should do, it also relieves organizations of doing a lot of other stuff they don't need to do."[3]

Noah held up his open left hand with the fingers and thumb all spread out, "Number five, 'Goals must have personal emotional involvement.'" Maury wondered how this one fit into the list with the rest but wrote 'involvement' to be slipped over the fifth step of the ladder.

Noah continued. "It is difficult to get excited about someone else's goal. If you get your employees involved in setting the goals or in the building of the plan of action it creates ownership. People tend to support what they help to create." The last sentence was stated with a strong down turn at the end as if he were quoting an old principle that applied to many situations.

Maury didn't know it but he would hear this sentence used over and over again in the next few weeks. He wrote it down in his notebook, underlined it twice and put a star on the edge of the paper to remind him to look at that again. "People tend to support what they help to create."[4]

---

[3] H. Norman Swarzkopf, *Operation Courage*, Leadership (Fall 1997).

[4] Ray Spies, Development Associates

*People tend to support what they help to create.

"Rule number six is, 'Goals must provide a meaningful reward.'" Noah's hand was cupped as if he had money in it, "The rewards the goal provides are the real reasons to go after the goal. Identify what the rewards of achieving the goal will be to everyone concerned."

While Maury put up the sixth rule he was thinking about what that reward might be. It might include some kind of celebration or something. He was still working on it in his mind but Noah was still going.

"The seventh one is, 'Go after one goal at a time.'" Noah had his index finger pointing toward the ceiling. "If people attempt to go after more than one or possibly two goals at a time, they can easily become frustrated, running in many different directions. Go after and concentrate on one or two goals at a time."

Maury agreed, "That is one of the biggest problems we have. We aren't focused." He recorded it, folded the paper and hung it on rung number seven.

Noah continued, " The last rule, number eight, is 'WAABO.'[5]

Maury squinted and asked, "Huh?"

"Walk Around And Be Observant. Inspect what you expect. Your people will be more likely to perform when they know you care enough to examine their progress."

---

[5] Improving Employee Productivity, Development Associates

Maury wrote 'WAABO' and hung the last folded paper on the top rung. "Okay, that's my assignment, 'write a goal that lives up to the eight rules.'" He started to set his tablet down.

"Well, there is a little more to it." Noah said with a smile.

Maury felt like he was being pushed a little here. Still, he wanted to actually get a result so he listened, paper and pencil in hand.

"After you have the goal written down it is time to break it down into bite sized pieces." Noah looked at Maury and asked, "Do you know how to eat an elephant?"

"No," laughed Maury.

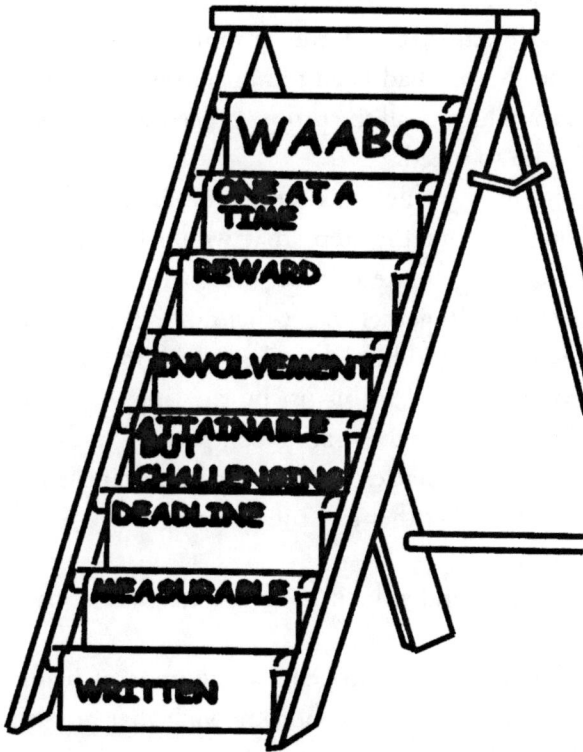

"One bite at a time," said Noah., pausing for effect, then continuing, "and that is how to achieve a goal as well.

"List the obstacles to overcome or the tasks that must be accomplished to have the goal materialize. It is not necessary to put them in any order now. Just write them as they come to mind."

Maury started thinking about the obstacles that were in the way of his goal. The goal is to meet the numerical goal which came on his daily printout. One thing that stood in the way was that his people didn't actually know he expected to reach the goal. He had been trying really hard to get there but hadn't actually sat down with them and talked with them about it. He wrote, "Let my team know that we are going to match the goal figure with actual."

Another obstacle was that Red, the new guy, wasn't quite up to the skill level they needed. Maury had been too busy trying to get the work done to take time to train him in all the proper procedures. He wrote that down too. "Bring Red up to speed."

As he thought, he was able to list several more obstacles.

He also thought about the steps that would be needed. He thought they should have a target date to meet the goal just one time first. They would all have to work together to get that done. He was sure they would learn something that would help them learn how to do it more often.

Several steps were added to his list by the time he got done thinking about it. He showed his list to Noah. Noah pointed to them with his pen, "Passing each of these obstacles and steps is important if you are to reach your overall goal. Let's call them all sub-goals."[6]

Maury nodded.

"Take each sub-goal and write it on a separate piece of paper." instructed Noah.

Maury quickly wrote the sub-goals at the tops of blank pages of his tablet. The first one was his team not knowing that he actually expected

---

[6] Bob Pecor, Development Associates

them to reach the plant goal. He wrote, "Tell my team what we are going to do," at the top of the first sheet. He continued, converting each obstacle into a small goal statement. He was careful to follow the eight rules for writing goals which he had learned just a little while ago.

"Sort the sub-goals. Put the one that should be done first on the top. The second one goes second, and so forth." Noah explained, "Then break each one down into the specific actions it will take to accomplish it. Assign each action a completion date and put the names of the people who will have to do something to get it done."

Maury looked up. He was getting the idea. "Thanks, Noah. I'll have this all together by…next Saturday?"

"No. Saturday is out. How about a week from tomorrow afternoon?" Noah said.

Goals of Significance

Maury mentally checked his calender and said, "Good."

As Noah was ascending the basement stairs Maury was already bent over his papers writing the action steps for his sub-goals.

His first sub-goal was to let the team know they were going to actually meet the goal. He would first have to set a meeting date. Then he would have to post the meeting plan. He decided it would be a good idea to meet at the pizza place after work, so he would need to talk to Mark about his plans and get permission.

It was well past lunch time when he got the lists done. He put them all into a folder and wrote, "Goals of Significance" on the cover. It was a step in the right direction.

Chapter VI

Communication and Conflict

It was Tuesday before Maury was able to get to Mark with his request to have a meeting.

"Mark?" Maury was knocking on the edge of the office door.

Mark held his hand up with the palm facing Maury. Maury could see that he had interrupted something. Mark bent over his work for about forty-five seconds before he looked up, obviously at a good stopping point. He smiled and said, "Come on in Maury."

Maury thought about the message conveyed by that gesture. It was a polite way to tell him to wait, yet didn't interrupt Mark's train of thought. Maury thought he might try it himself. "Mark, I want to have a meeting with my work team. I've been working on some goals and wanted to talk to them about it."

Mark brightened at his announcement and said, "Sounds like a great idea. How can I help?"

Maury was uncertain. He wasn't sure what was okay to ask for and what wasn't. He suddenly realized he wasn't sure what he was going to say, "Well, I guess, uh I mean, well…to tell the truth…"

Mark interrupted, "I've never heard such a string of weasel words[7] in one sentence."

"Weasel words?" Maury questioned.

"The weasel removes the inside of eggs, leaving the structure of the shell intact. Weasel words leave the structure of a sentence grammatically correct, but weaken the meaning of it," answered Mark. "The words you use help to create the image people have of you."

---

[7] Improving Employee Productivity, Development Associates

"I'll try to be more prepared next time," said Maury.

"Try?" mused Mark.

"Whoops, another weasel word," said Maury, obviously embarrassed.

"You are a strategic link in the communication process," said Mark. "Often you are the only link between upper management and front line employees."

Maury changed the subject only slightly, "Maybe you could give me some pointers about leading a meeting with my team. As I said, I want to talk with my work team about some goals. Do you have any suggestions that would help me?" He was getting back to what had brought him there in the first place.

Mark put the tips of his fingers and thumbs together and said thoughtfully, "Well, the first thing is to decide what you want the outcome to be. Ask yourself, 'What result do I want?' 'What impression do I want to make?' and then, 'How can I best get the result I want?' and be sure you come in with an agenda prepared in advance. That will help you keep the meeting on track."

Maury thought of the lesson he had learned from Noah. He said, half under his breath, "Result drives process."

"That's it exactly." said Mark.

"What else should I know?" Maury asked.

"Maury, never forget that communication is a two way street. Too many people get all caught up in what they want to say and the result they want and forget that there are at least two people in every conversation. True respect for your team is demonstrated by listening to them and including their contribution in decision making. After all, people tend to support what they help to create."

In his mind Maury underlined that phrase again. "People tend to support what they help to create."

Maury asked, "What do you think about my idea of meeting with my team off site? I was thinking about the Pizza Place."

"Sounds like a good idea. We have some funds that are reserved for staff development. Go ahead and set it up and the plant will pick up the tab. Go easy on it," said Mark.

Maury felt great as he made his way out to the floor to see how his work team was doing. It seemed that the heavy burden he had picked up when he started this position was getting lighter.

"Everybody listen up." He got their attention. "We're going to have a meeting. It will be at the Pizza Place tomorrow right after work." He paused a moment and hearing no objection said, "Okay, back to work." He decided to disregard the sideways glance and frown on Linda's face.

"That wasn't so hard," he thought.

Little did he know that he had just opened up a whole can of worms.

As the shift was finishing, Maury again reminded them of the meeting the next night. Linda looked at him and said, "Hope you have a good time at your meeting. I ain't givin' up my free time just to get yelled at by the brass."

Maury was floored. "What's your problem?" He reacted.

"What's yours?" Linda mumbled over her shoulder. Then she was out the door.

As Maury drove home he thought about what had just happened. The weight was back. When he pulled into the driveway he saw Noah over in the yard behind Noah's house. Maury saw that he was whittling on a greying old oak stick. "Excuse me." Maury called across the yard.

"Maury," He responded. "How's it going?"

That was just the opening Maury was hoping for. He said, "Got a couple of minutes?"

"Sure," said Noah. Soon they were both sitting on overturned buckets under the oak tree. Noah handed one of his carving knives to Maury. "What's the trouble."

Maury told Noah about his meeting announcement and the backfire it caused. He told about how he felt angry, defensive and embarrassed.

Noah said, "Do you want to get even? Or do you want to resolve the conflict?" He always seemed to get right to the point.

Maury held up his oak stick. He had whittled it nearly away. He looked at his sliver of a stick as if he was looking at his employee. "Part of me wants to get back at her. Don't I deserve some respect as the team leader?"

Noah left the rhetorical question unanswered as Maury continued. "But I know it is important for the sake of the team and the company that I handle this right and not blow up."

"What result do you want?" Noah asked.

Maury thought a while and answered, "I want my people to understand me. I want to make the team better, not worse. Linda just wasn't listening. If I could just get her to listen to me I'm sure I can work this out."

"Do you think she's ready to listen and work things out?" Noah asked.

"No," answered Maury. "I think I'm in for a big fight. I am afraid I will end up having to do something drastic like fire her or something. Do you know any way to avoid it?" His stick was too small to whittle any more and he let it fall among the shavings.

Noah held up his carving and looked at it with one eye closed. He had made a chess piece, a knight. "There are only four possible ways to address a conflict. The first one is 'lose-win'. That means you give in. You lose and she wins."

Maury didn't like the sound of that and waited for the next one.

Noah continued, "The second one is compromise."

Maury liked that one a little better. He had been taught as a child that compromise was a very noble thing to do.

Noah was still describing the second option. "With compromise neither one of you wins. It is called 'lose-lose'."

When Noah called it 'lose-lose' Maury didn't like the sound of it nearly so well. It didn't seem like such a good idea any more.

"Then there is the 'win-lose' option," said Noah. That is where you go in loaded with your agenda and fight for your side. You make sure you win and she loses." As he said that Noah was looking right in Maury's eyes.

Maury thought this must be the one he would have to take. It wasn't comfortable, but as a boss he had a responsibility to maintain discipline.

He said, "You said there were four ways to address a conflict. Tell me about the last one."

Noah said, "The fourth way is the 'win-win' choice. That is where both of you come out winners."

Maury spoke. "I have had experience with the first three. None of them seems like one I would willingly choose. I don't want to be the loser. That eliminates the first two. And I don't want to be mean spirited either. That puts number three in the 'last resort' category. Tell me about number four."

He remembered the lesson he had learned earlier and thought, "If it is true that result drives the process, then before I address the conflict I had better decide what result I want. I need to decide the result before I choose the method I will use."

Noah shifted his seat on the plastic bucket and picked up four sticks about the size of short pencils. "The 'win-win' conflict resolution method requires careful attention to the following steps. They must be taken in order, one at a time, and each step must be completed before you go on to the next one." His voice sounded very serious.

"Step one is in your head." Noah said as he gave Maury one of the sticks. "You have to go into the conversation with an attitude that both of you can come out winners. Think 'win-win'[8]. When you address the conflict, open up the conversation with a statement like, 'I know we have a problem,' and keep the 'win-win' in your head."

Maury looked at the first stick and gripped it. Thinking 'win-win'. That one wasn't so hard. He used his carving knife and shaved a smooth place on the side of the stick. Then he took his pen and wrote, "Win-win Attitude" on the smooth white oak.

"Step two comes from one of the sayings of James the Less and is almost two thousand years old, 'Be quick to listen and slow to speak'."[9] Noah gave Maury the second stick. "That means that you must listen first.

---

[8] Stephen R. Covey, First Things First, Simon &Schuster, New York, 1994

[9] Holy Bible: New International Version, Zondervan Bible Publishers, 1984

Say to Linda, 'I want to make sure I understand you. You have your say first'. When she has spoken, paraphrase the story she has told and ask, 'Have I got it right?' You have to be patient and make sure you are able to tell her story to her satisfaction."

Maury thought about his reaction minutes before. He had just wanted Linda to understand him. He hadn't been thinking at all about understanding her. Noah could have been reading his mind.

As Maury shaved a smooth place to write toward one end of the stick Noah continued, "Make sure you get her side first. 'Quick to listen' means make sure you understand her side before you give your's. You earn the right to speak by listening first."

Maury wrote the phrase, "Quick to Listen," on the left as he held the side of the stick facing him.

"The other half of the second step is 'slow to speak'. When you have listened and made sure she is satisfied that you understand her, then you can say, 'Okay, let me tell you my point of view. Does that sound fair enough?' It is a way to open up your side of the story. Again, be patient and make sure you aren't insisting that Linda agrees with you, just that she understands where you are coming from." As Noah explained Maury wrote the last phrase.

Maury held the two sticks in his hand and repeated in his mind, "First have a win-win attitude. Second, be quick to listen and slow to speak."

Noah held out the third stick and said, "The old saying has another phrase, '…slow to become angry.' You avoid an angry fight by identifying the points where you will disagree. You say, 'Let's identify where we disagree.' Then you write down each point of disagreement. Both of you get to contribute to the list."

Maury took the third stick. He could imagine several points of disagreement between himself and Linda. As he had with the others, he shaved the side of the stick smooth. He wrote, "anger," and fished a red pen from his shirt pocket. He drew an oblong circle around the word and a slash diagonally through it thinking, "That should remind me to keep my anger out of the way." Then he wrote, "Points of disagreement."

"When both of you are satisfied with the list, you set it aside and go on to step four."

This didn't sound logical to Maury. He thought, "Where is the place where I argue and decide who wins? When do I get to use logic to change her mind?" He said, "If I am just going to set the points of disagreement aside what's the point of writing them down. Why do it if I'm not going to use them?"

"They do have a use," said Noah. "They are used as a door stop. You use them to keep the door open for the next step. If you don't do that they will be like a brick on the sidewalk. Both of you will trip over them and never get to the solution. This is the 'win-win' solution, not the 'win-lose' one."

Noah went on, "The last step is creating a mutual solution. With the points of disagreement set aside you both have a responsibility to work together and find a solution that is satisfactory to both of you." He handed Maury the last stick.

Win-Win Attitude

Quick to listen | **Slow to speak**

Points of disagreement

Create a Mutual Solution

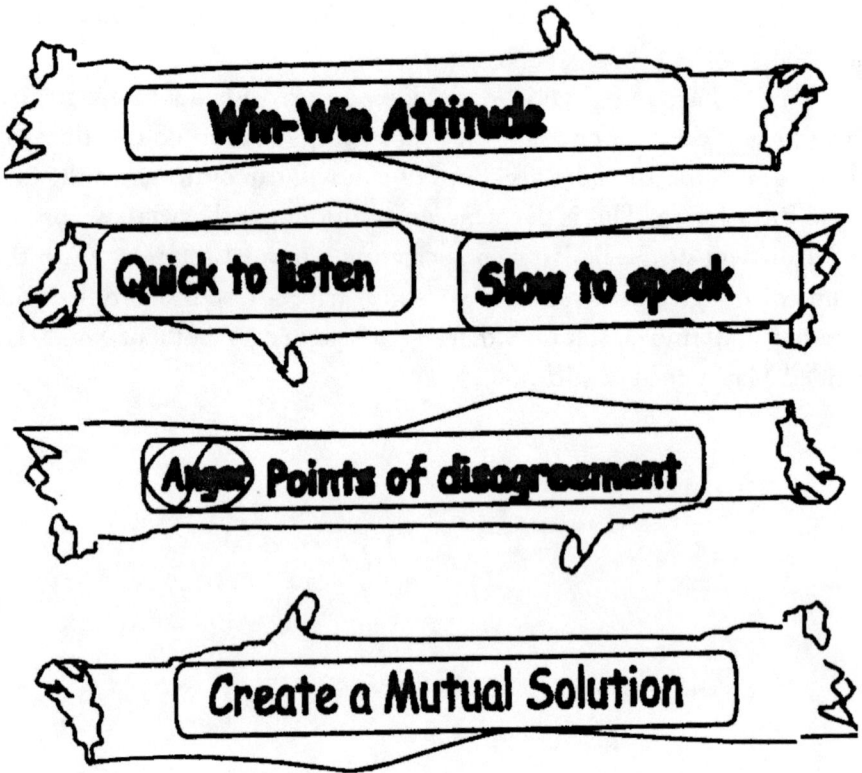

It sounded like it should work. He shaved the side of the stick and wrote, "Create a mutual solution." Maury thanked Noah and put the sticks in his pocket. He worried about what would happen the next day so he read the sticks over several times before bed.

On Wednesday morning he met Linda at the door first thing. She looked defensive but Maury knew he had to take care of this. He said, "Linda, we have to talk," motioning toward an office. "Let's sit down together and work this out."

He reached in his pocket, took out the four small sticks and held them in his hand. They weren't obvious but for him it was a way to remember the steps.

He shifted the first one back to his pocket thinking, "We can both be winners." He was making sure he had the win-win attitude.

Linda complied with his request and stepped into the office. He followed her in.

She spoke right away and said, "I'm listening." But her folded arms and pursed lips told him she wasn't ready to hear anything. He could see her eyes roll and understood the wisdom of 'quick to listen'. He could see that if he tried to make her understand him first, they wouldn't get anywhere. She would roll her eyes some more, argue, maybe give in, and there would be bad blood between them for a long time.

"Linda, let me make sure I understand your point of view." He said it just like he had rehearsed it the night before. He held the second stick loosely as he spoke.

Linda still seemed defensive but started to tell her point. He stayed with it, restating and paraphrasing her story until she agreed that he really did understand her point of view.

She was angry that he had gotten the job she wanted. She thought he was also mad at her. She didn't like to see him acting like a boss when he had been her equal up until very recently.

He resisted arguing against her story. He didn't make any comments when it seemed she had misunderstood his purpose. It was hard not to comment but he was determined to follow the steps as Noah had laid them out. He had been very insistent that the steps be followed precisely and in the order he gave them.

When she was satisfied that he really understood, he went on to the next half of step two. Putting the sticks in his pocket as he completed each step, he was relieved when they got past the points of disagreement.

When it came to creating the mutual solution, it wasn't very hard at all. It was just a matter of shifting the timing of the meeting around to avoid causing trouble with her babysitter. It was a good solution for both of them.

She went to get started on the shipping line and Maury slipped in a little late for the morning team leader meeting. He felt like he had just gotten his sea legs. The shipping and receiving floor felt a little more steady that day.

Chapter VII

Leading a Meeting

Later that morning Maury stopped at Mark's office to let him know about the meeting plans with his team.

"Got everything all worked out? Mark asked.

Maury was thinking of his interaction with Linda and said, "Yes, it took a little rearranging of schedules but everything is set for tonight."

Mark said, "That's not what I mean. I was asking about how you plan to conduct the meeting itself." Mark held his head at a slight angle as he waited for Maury's response.

Maury was taken by surprise by that statement. He hadn't considered the actual meeting itself. He had just thought he would eat pizza with his team and at some time during the meeting, get their attention and tell them his goal setting plans and ask if they had any ideas to add. "I don't really know," Maury said. "I guess I'll just wing it."

Mark's expression said that wasn't a good idea. He said, "Maury, let's make some plans for your meeting tonight."

Maury pulled up a chair to the table in Mark's office. He opened his pad of paper and took out his pen. "Sounds like a good idea."

Mark started with a question, "Why are you going to meet?"

Maury thought, "Result drives process, of course." He said, "The purpose of my meeting is to let my workers know about some goals I am developing for them." He wrote the purpose on the top of his paper.

Mark asked, "Are you going to include them in the goal setting process?"

Maury answered, "I hadn't really thought about that part. But now that you mention it, I think it is a good idea."

Mark leaned forward. "The first step in planning for a meeting is to set the agenda."

Maury said, "I know that an agenda is a list of things that will be talked about in a meeting. However, I always thought that you didn't need to do that when the meeting is not a formal occasion."

Mark said, "Even though you are meeting in a casual setting, the purpose of the meeting is important. It is company business and deserves the same attention you would give a formal meeting."

Maury could see that the meeting had the potential to do more than he had previously expected. Mark continued, "If the meeting is one where you want input from your people you need to make sure you take advantage of every brain in the room."

"How do you do that?" asked Maury.

"There are several things that can add to the mental power in a meeting. The first is to switch on all the brains well ahead of time so they have time to warm up."

Maury must have looked puzzled because Mark explained. "That means getting a meeting announcement out ahead of time so people can think about the subject they will have to work on. For some meetings you will want to give assignments to your people to gather information that will be used to help you with the team decision making."

Maury asked, checking, "When I give my team an opportunity to think about the meeting and work on it in advance it is switching on all the brains. Right?" Seeing Mark nod, Maury wrote, 'Post an announcement.'

Mark watched what he wrote and said, "Be sure the announcement contains the subjects that the team will be discussing. Encourage your people to talk about the subject before the meeting. People will naturally want to do this but sometimes feel like they are seeking or cheating if they talk outside the meeting. Encouraging them to talk outside the meeting gives them permission and helps people feel better about the pre-meeting discussions which others have."

They bent over the table working. Soon Maury had a list including instructions on planning, establishing an agenda, setting dates and times, and preparing the participants.

Mark said, "Maury, you have some responsibilities in leading a meeting that you did not have before you were in a position of leadership. You must be organized, maintain order. Keep the meeting upbeat and start and end the meeting on time." Maury was busy writing and didn't look up.

"I have a couple of techniques that will help make your meeting a success," Mark said. "The first is a way of generating meeting rules that your people will like. The second is a team decision making process." Mark described the techniques while Maury took notes.

> *"Most people are*
> *unaware of what their*
> *nonverbal communication*
> *is saying."*[10]

Evening came and Maury pulled up at the Pizza Place. It was later than he had originally planned, having worked out a revised meeting time with Linda. He saw Red and John arriving in John's sporty old car. They each carried a copy of the meeting announcement which Maury had distributed.

Maury was nervous. He didn't know why. These were the same people he worked with every day. Yet the occasion of a meeting made the experience a new one.

The Pizza Place had given them a room which allowed them to sit around the outsides of tables in a 'u' shape. It had a nice big white board on the wall. Maury relaxed just a little during the meal. Never-the-less, he made sure he ate less than he would have if he wasn't going to lead the meeting. When they were pretty well done he stood and started the meeting.

"Welcome to our first meeting since I have been privileged to be your team leader." He was trying to set the stage. Their expressions said he was doing okay. "Since this is our first meeting I thought it would be a good idea to set a few meeting rules."

---

[10]Earnest G. Beier, Psychology Today (October 1974).

Their expressions showed that they weren't particularly interested in this part. He continued, "Tell me about the worst and the best meetings you have been in."

Silence stared back at him. He waited. Then to his relief, Linda spoke, "I always hate it when one person hogs the floor all the time." Maury opened a marker and wrote her concern on the whiteboard.

Red added, "I like it when we stick to the subject, not getting off into side conversations."

Maury continued writing as everyone joined in. After a few minutes there was a list of what his people liked and didn't like in meetings. He asked, "Do you think these would be good rules for us to live by when we have meetings?"

They did. Maury asked for a volunteer to take notes. John agreed to do it, "I'll take notes this time if it doesn't mean I have to do it every time we have a meeting." They all agreed that the task of note taking would be changed when they had future meetings. John asked, "What kind of notes do we need?"

Maury explained what he had learned from Mark earlier in the day, "You don't have to record all the conversation or discussion. Just write down the decisions we make, action plans, names of people who will do something and dates we set." John was ready to do that.

Maury addressed the team, "The purpose of our meeting is to set some team goals." He went on to explain that he wanted to achieve more than they had before. Then he said, "What are your ideas about how to reach these goals?"

The team was a little slow getting started but Maury encouraged them all to participate, writing their contributions on the board. Soon there were several good ideas listed. Maury listed the steps and obstacles on individual sheets. He assigned groups of two to three to work through each sub-goal and write action plans. Soon they came to agreement about how to reach the goals.

Maury said, "There is one more thing we need to do. Mark says we should never close a meeting without sewing up the bottom of the bag."

They looked as confused as Maury had been when Mark explained it to him. Maury drew a picture of a big feed bag, the kind used to hold animal feed, "This feed bag represents our meeting. We have filled it full of important decisions. Before we pick it up and carry it out of the room, we need to make sure we sew up the bottom. If we don't, everything we have put into the bag will fall out. The way we keep from losing all the benefit of our meeting is to take care of the accountability steps."

Maury continued, "Let's list the actions we have agreed to do." He asked John to read from his notes the actions they had decided on. "Beside each action we need a name of the person responsible to carry it out and the deadline for getting it done. After that write down the method we will use to follow-up to see if the action is successful."

Red said, "Put me down for that first action." Then he gave a date that he would carry it out. Soon the rest had joined in, each taking a part.

After the meeting, Linda stopped Maury, "Not a bad meeting. Not like the meetings I have seen where it seems like no body gets anything done."

Maury said, "I'm still learning. Mark was a great help in showing me how to make sure the meeting accomplishes its purpose through the accountability steps."

Linda asked, "Are we going to have more meetings?"

Maury said, "I'm sure we will. I have begun to learn that people tend to support what they help to create."

Linda said, "It sure feels better when we are asked to participate in deciding how to reach our goals rather than just being told what to do. I liked being able to give my ideas. I have had them for quite a while but I didn't think anybody up there wanted to hear it."

Mark said, "I'll see you at work tomorrow."

On the way home he wondered why so many managers and team leaders don't take advantage of the thinking skills of their people.

The next morning Maury made copies of the action plans, names of the people who had responsibilities and the deadline dates for completion. He gave one to Mark, kept one for himself and passed the rest out to his team. As he gave out the copies he felt that he was distributing the weight of responsibility throughout his team. It was a successful feeling. He was getting the work done and using the strength of the whole team to do it.

Chapter VIII

Group Problem Solving

Saturday found Maury exhausted. He slept late that morning and got behind and didn't really get any more done on his basement bathroom. Sunday afternoon he showed up at Noah's house next door for his coaching session.

Noah waved him to the kitchen door as he came up the steps. Even before he got to the door he caught the enticing aroma of cookies baking.

"Thanks for your help with my communication problem," Maury said. "And I held my first team meeting. Mark gave me some help and..." Maury went on to tell Noah all about the meeting.

"You don't look too beat up from it all," grinned Noah. "Would you like some oatmeal cookies?"

"Sure," said Maury. "They smell great!"

"Well you will have to wait a little while. They aren't quite ready," said Noah.

"Thanks a lot," laughed Maury. "You get my saliva flowing with anticipation and then you make me wait."

Noah switched topics on the fly. "Maury, how often do you plan to hold your team meetings?"

"I'm not sure," Maury said. "It was a good meeting but I know the company won't spring for pizza for my people very often. I suppose we can do it every month or so." He sound like he might not be able to actually do it that often.

"But I thought you said it was really productive," said Noah.

Maury responded, "Yeah, but they don't want us to spend too much time in meetings, time away from actual production."

"If you could do anything you wanted, how often would you like to be able to hold highly productive meetings with your people that would tap into their thinking to improve your operations?" Noah asked with that look in his eye that told Maury he was in for a great coaching session.

Maury had learned by now to just go ahead and say what he was thinking. "Well, I suppose I would like to be able to stop and hold a meeting several times a month as new problems appear. But that would shut down the operation and cause problems for all the other departments."

"So you need to be able to find a way to hold a meeting when you don't have time to hold a meeting?" asked Noah.

"Okay?" said Maury tentatively, feeling like he had been led into this one. "How do you do that?"

"First," said Noah, "do you know how to go through the basic group problem solving process?"

Maury thought back to his school days and pulled up a tried and true method he picked up somewhere. "I remember the basic steps. Identify the problem; brainstorm for possible solutions; select the best one; and implement."

Noah said, "That is a good precise view of problem solving and would serve you well no matter what other kinds of techniques you may want to plug into it. The trick is doing it without pulling your people away from their jobs."

"Right," said Maury wrinkling his brow as he thought. "Is that possible?"

"It is," answered Noah with characteristic cheerfulness. "Since you know the basic steps of group problem solving, see if you can think of which steps must be done in a meeting and which can be done without a meeting."

Maury paused and reflected before answering. "I have never tried this before, but it seems to me that I could at least start to identify the problem without a meeting. After all, I wouldn't even call a meeting if I didn't have a problem to start off with."

"Good thinking," said Noah. "You discover a problem even before you call the meeting.

What about selecting the specific people you want to work on the problem?"

"I don't see why not," Maury said. "If I have identified the problem, I could easily select the team members who would be right for that problem without calling the whole team together. I might have to ask around a bit, but I think I would have to do that even if I called them all together."

Noah threw in another question, "Do you think you could announce the problem as a subject before the meeting?"

"Sure!" said Maury. "I could put it in the news letter, post it on the bulletin board or tell each person in the team individually."

"Okay," said Noah. "Now let's work on developing the problem a little. I have found that most problem solving efforts that get into trouble, get into trouble because the problem is not clearly enough understood or agreed on by members of the team. After you select the topic and choose the team members and let them know what the topic is, the next step is to ask a question."

"What question do I need to ask?" queried Maury.

"Ask them what they think the real problem is," said Noah. "That gets your people to start thinking deeper and gets them digging for root causes, the underlying conditions that cause the problems."

"I think I could do that before the meeting starts too," said Maury excitedly. "I could go to them one at a time and ask what they think the real problem is and get their answers before the meeting ever starts."

Noah added, "Every part of the group problem solving process which can be completed one-to-one, saves the time of the group."

Maury responded, "I can see how that would save time but when do I need to bring the people together, Noah?"

"After you get input from everyone on the true nature of the problem," Noah said, "you need to call your people together for a few minutes to clarify the focus of your problem solving effort. Huddle for a few minutes, share the input you have gathered from all the team members and come to an agreement on what specific problem your team will solve. Once you have done that, you may dismiss your people."

"What about the solution?" asked Maury.

"That is the very next step." Noah answered. "Again you go to your team members one at a time and ask them for suggestions for the solution. Since they are not confined to a meeting, you can give them time to think on it for a while."

Maury said, "That's not the way I expected it to be done. Usually I have seen meetings in which people talked over the problem and thought of the solutions together."

Just then Maury heard the oven timer ring.

Noah said, "I think the cookies are ready," getting up and stepping to the oven. He opened the oven door and using a pad, took out a cookie sheet of hot oatmeal cookies. He used a spatula to transfer them to a plate.

The first one Maury tasted was so hot he could only take a little bite. "These are great. What's your secret?"

Noah said, "I think the secret is waiting. You have to let the dough rest in the refrigerator for a while before you put them on the cookie sheet, and then you have to time the baking just right.

"Actually, that is the way it is with problem solving. A lot of people just jump right into the search for the solution. That prevents their people from talking it over with others and from doing research or consulting with people who have expertise or experience. If you want higher quality thinking, you have to give people time to let their ideas cook a while. Depending on the nature of the problem you may want to give them day or a week to work on it so their decisions don't come out half baked."

"Well, it sure seems to work well with cookies," Maury chuckled.

Noah continued, "After you get individual input from your team on possible solutions, pull them together again to make a decision."

"I can hardly wait to try this one out," said Maury. "I am guessing that is my next assignment. Am I right?"

"Yes, but before we leave the group problem solving meeting, there is one last part that needs to be done." Noah said.

Maury hesitated a moment and brightened as he spoke, "The accountability steps?"

Noah smiled. "That's right. For this kind of meeting, when you are trying to minimize the time you spend in meetings, you may want to make the assignments yourself. Just write them down with the names, actions, dates, reporting methods and rewards and consequences. Then distribute the assignments and follow up to make sure it all gets done on time."

Maury said, "I'll do it this week."

Noah said, "It seems to me that every team leader should have this kind of a problem solving project going all the time. It is a way to harness the stray thoughts and the thinking power of your people."

"How about next week at the same time?" asked Maury, wanting to be sure he scheduled his coaching on a regular basis.

Noah said, "That would work out fine. See you then.

Chapter IX

Training Your People

Maury held a group problem solving meeting just like he and Noah had gone over in his coaching session. It started on Monday. He gathered input into the deeper nature of the problem on Tuesday, let them think over the solutions until Thursday and held an early afternoon huddle meeting to decide on the solution on Friday. Before they all left Friday evening, each one had an assignment sheet with actions and dates and everything

By the time Saturday arrived Maury was energized. He got up early and made great progress on the bathroom project. He got the plumbing all stubbed in and the plasterboard up and ready for taping.

On Sunday afternoon he took his pad and pen and went next door for his coaching session. Noah was in the garage sweeping up wood shavings when Maury arrived.

Maury gave Noah a quick report on his group problem solving meeting and said, "The next goal I have is to increase the skills of my team."

"Before we get to that, I was wondering how your bathroom project was coming along." Noah said unexpectedly. He shoved an overturned bucket toward Maury and sat on an old folding chair himself.

"I have the plumbing in the walls and the sheet rock up. I'm ready to cover the nails and cracks," Maury responded as he took his seat on the bucket. He was sure Noah had something up his sleeve.

"Do you know anything about sheet rock taping?" Noah asked.

"Yeah, I learned last summer when my dad came to visit and we fixed up the attic room." Maury answered.

"Maury, do you remember how your dad taught you to sheet rock?" Noah was leaning forward and listening carefully.

"Well, I do remember that we had a hard time getting along," said Maury. "I felt like a little kid again. It wasn't all that much fun. But I learned eventually."

Noah continued, attentively, "What made it so difficult, Maury?"

"Well Dad just told me to get started and he would tell me when I was wrong." answered Maury. "I spent the whole rest of the day listening to him tell me how stupid I was, how I should have a brain, and how I should know not to do it like that. I didn't really have any idea what he wanted."

Noah nodded in understanding, "Training is like that in a lot of workplaces. People are told to go do things they don't know how to do. Then they are berated when they don't do it right."

"I guess it is like the process-result question. I was jumping right into the process without any understanding of the result he wanted," said Maury. "I can see that there are definitely some things I don't want to do. Can you give me some coaching on the training process?"

"I think I can help," said Noah. "Take out your paper there and draw five small pictures."

Maury whipped out his paper and was ready without hesitation.

Noah said, "First draw a heart."

Maury made a little valentine just like one he had carved in a tree when he was a kid to show his best girl how he felt about her.

Noah said, "The first step is: Teach it to their heart."

Maury's puzzled look prompted Noah to continue, "You have to tell them the big reason, the great things this new task leads to or supports. Tell them about the mission of the company and how this new task fits into the big picture. If you don't, the training doesn't seem important. And if it doesn't seem important, it will be boring. And if it is boring, they won't listen well and won't learn well."

Maury said, "So you teach it to their heart by helping them love it."

"That's exactly right," said Noah. "I couldn't have said it better myself."

He continued, "The next two items often go together. Draw an eye and an ear."

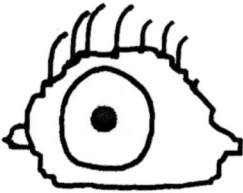

Maury quickly drew the pictures as directed.

Noah explained, "Second, you teach it to their eye and third you teach it to their ear. That is, you show and tell them how to do the new task."

Maury understood these two steps and nodded his head thoughtfully.

"Next," said Noah, "draw a hand."

Maury drew an open hand with the palm facing forward.

Noah explained the symbol, "The fourth step is to let them try their hand."

Maury added, "That means I should give them a chance to try out their new skill."

Noah confirmed Maury's conclusion, "Yes."

Maury said, "You said there were five pictures. It looks like we are finished after four."

Noah said, "There is one more. The last picture is a mouth."

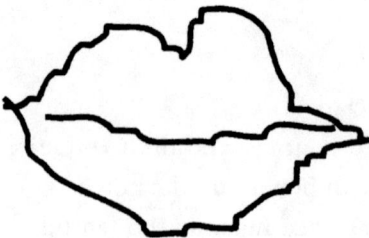

Maury drew a mouth on his paper and looked down at the list of drawings.

1.

2.

3.

4.

5.

"The last step is called 'teach back,'" said Noah. "It is the guarantee of learning. Many people try to bluff their way though the learning process hoping they will pick up what they missed at a later time. That often leaves them short of the critical skills needed. The 'teach back' method insures that the trainee has really learned the new skill."

"You mean you ask the new trainee to teach their new skill back to the trainer?" asked Maury.

"That's exactly what I mean," answered Noah. You first teach their heart, then their eye and their ear, then their hand, and finally you teach it to their mouth.

"How much better would it have been if your father had first shown you what the finished job was supposed to turn out like, then showed you and told you how to do the job, and let you try your hand until you felt comfortable and then finally asked you explain it all back to him just to make sure you had it all right?"

Maury thought about that and said, "I think my training would have gone a whole lot more smoothly and my sheet rock job would have been smoother too."

Then Maury asked, "Is there any order in which employees should receive training? Are there some parts that should be put ahead of others?"

"Sure," Noah said. "Take your paper there and write the following categories leaving space to fill in some ideas. At the top of the page write the name of one of your people whom you want to train."

Maury wrote 'Red' at the top of the page.

"Write the name of his position beside the name," Noah said. "Then use the rest of the page to cover these three categories: essential responsibilities, secondary responsibilities, and cross-training objectives."

Maury wrote down the position, ' packer'. Under that he wrote the categories. Then he began to fill in the spaces.

Noah said, "You will be able to see that your employee already has some of the skills. Others skills need a little help and some are completely beyond his present skill level. The essential responsibilities are the first priority. The employee will not be satisfactory to you nor feel satisfied himself without mastery of these skills. After these are gained you can move to secondary responsibilities and cross-training objectives. They will need to be scheduled in order of the contribution which can be made to the overall company objectives."

Maury was writing notes as Noah talked. He was taken by surprise by the next question.

"Maury, who is responsible for training your people?"

Maury was quick to answer. "Well I am, of course. As team leader it's my responsibility to make sure my people have the skills they need to do their job. It says that in my job description."

Noah followed up, "And who is responsible to do the training?"

Maury was confused. He thought the question was the same as the one before. "I'm not sure I know what you mean."

Noah said, "I know you said you are responsible to make sure your people are trained, but does that mean you have to do it yourself?"

"No, I guess not," stammered Maury. Then with more confidence, "I think the people who are doing the jobs now could do some of the training."

"And," said Noah, "how would you go about preparing them for the responsibility?"

Maury thought about that for a minute and said, "It seems to me that my new trainers should be trained in training techniques in the same way the trainees are trained in the new skills."

Noah said, "Mind putting that in English?" His smile opened the way for Maury to explain more clearly.

"Well, training is a skill. If I want my best people to train others, I need to teach them training skills." Maury responded.

"I would need to teach the training skills by first showing them the great effect good training can have on the person they train. Then I should let them watch me do the some training while giving them an explanation of how training is done. Then they would be ready to try their hand at training on some task they are familiar with. Finally I would have them confirm their learning by practicing. They could practice by teaching me the training method they just learned."

"What would that do for people in your team that have a desire to move up in the organization?" Noah asked.

Maury felt like a light bulb switched on over his head. "It could be part of a skill improvement program that would help them build a career track." He had already decided to see if Linda would take on some of the training responsibility. Maybe her ambitions could be a benefit to the company as well as to her.

Chapter X

Motivating the People

For the next several weeks Maury was occupied setting up folders for each of his people. It included a full set of competencies associated with each of their jobs. Next was a chart to track their progress toward mastering them. After that was an individual training schedule. He felt like he had truly moved more toward the planning part of his leadership responsibility and was having to do much less of the controlling behaviors. The long handled tools made him feel much more successful.

Meanwhile Maury's bathroom project had stalled. He had done the taping and gotten most of the fixtures in place, but didn't have the bathtub he wanted. He was hoping for one of those old tubs with legs.

It was early Saturday morning when he heard Noah's old Ford pickup pulling into Maury's driveway. He jumped out of bed and rushed to the window to see what was going on. Noah was getting out and looking back toward the back of the truck. There in the bed of the truck was an old bathtub.

Maury hurried into his clothes and was half way down the steps when Noah rang the bell.

"Noah, what's going on?" Maury asked.

"I hope I didn't disturb you," Noah said, "but I was out at an old farm auction and found this great tub. I remembered there was a tub on your project list and took a chance that you might like this one."

With his feet still in slippers Maury went out and circled the bed of the pickup, speechless. It had all four legs, some stains on the porcelain that looked very removable and brass fixtures which matched the ones he was using in his bathroom project. Then he spoke, "It's great. How much did it cost?"

Noah answered, "Got it for seventy-five bucks. If you want it for that, it's yours. Otherwise I'm stuck with an old tub." He was obviously proud of his acquisition.

"Sure." Maury said. He made out a check right there and gave it to Noah. "Now, how are we going to get it out of the truck and into the basement? That thing looks like it weighs nine hundred pounds."

"We are going to have to have some help I think," said Noah. "It took four guys to lift it into the truck."

"It reminds me of the situation at work," said Maury.

"How's that?" asked Noah.

Maury requested, "I need some help lifting the morale of my team."

"Let's talk about that." said Noah.

Maury went on, "With your help getting my sea legs I am managing to meet the production goal about eighty percent of the time," said Maury. "The natural fluctuations in production make it impossible to stay on a straight line, so I want to start exceeding the goal on some of the days to make up for the ones where we don't quite get there."

"You have reached the target you set a few weeks ago," questioned Noah, "and are ready to raise the bar?"

Maury answered, "Just like the pole vault at the Olympics. We want to go higher. I did like I did before, set the goal, made the plans and let everybody know what was expected but it seems like the steam is all gone out of them…"

"They just don't seem to be excited about it," he continued. "They are about as hard to move as this tub."

"It is interesting that you use that comparison. Look at the word 'motivation'." With his finger Noah traced the word into the dust on the fender of the old Ford pickup.

motivation

Noah underlined the first part of the word and added a little 'e' after the 'v.' Then he underline the second half and crowded a 'c' in before the second 't.'

<u>motiv_eaction</u>

He said, "You will notice that it looks like two words, 'motive' and 'action'. Your people have to have a motive for action."

"There are two kinds of motivation." Noah said as he pointed to the bed of the pickup.

"One kind is a motivational floor. This is one kind of force. It is like the bed of this truck. It has to be strong and stable to keep the tub from breaking through and falling on the road. This kind of motivation keeps people satisfied."

"You mean it keeps people from quitting?" asked Maury.

Noah answered, "Some people quit and leave. Others quit and don't leave."

Maury laughed, "That's for sure."

Noah continued, "This kind of motivation is like the temperature in the room. If the temperature is within a certain range it is comfortable. There is nothing you can do to heighten a person's pleasure by adjusting the temperature."

Maury asked, "Can you give me an example?"

"I can give you several," said Noah. "Some things that fit into that category are wages, security, fairness, opportunity to socialize, and safe comfortable work conditions. These factors all make it possible for your people to continue to work. If they are missing, it has a negative effect on their ability to perform."

Maury asked, "How would I know if there was a problem in these areas?"

Noah responded, "There are a lot of symptoms of this problem. Some of them would be work slowdowns, increased complaints, petty arguing and high turnover. If these problems are present you need to look at changing the factors that cause them."

Maury looked at the floor of the pickup and said, "I think the motivational floor is okay. The problem with my employees is they don't get excited about their work. When I talked about higher goals they just kept on working like they were before. I know they could do more if they just wanted it a little more."

Noah climbed up into the pickup, squatted down and gripped the curved edge of the tub. He staggered as he attempted to straighten up with the heavy load. Through his teeth he said, "It takes a completely different kind of force to lift the tub."

He set it down and, breathing heavily, said, "You can strengthen the floor all you want but that won't lift the tub any higher."

Maury could see the difference between the two kinds of force. He asked, "What kind of force will raise the motivation of my team to work harder and get more accomplished?"

Noah climbed down and laid his hand on Maury's shoulder. "That, my friend, is a horse of a different color. If you are wanting people to work harder and put more of themselves into the work, you have to use a completely different category of motivation."

Maury invited Noah into the kitchen and got his tablet and pen. He said, "Noah, I want to know what these magic motivators are."

Noah said, "There are a bunch of them. One is recognition for accomplishment. People will work harder when they know they will be recognized for their skills, abilities and effort.

"Another motivator is the feeling of accomplishment itself. That is an inner feeling that they are reaching new heights. People will exert extra effort when their work is challenging.

"Some people respond to increased responsibility and others to a sense of importance. When you can give them greater access to information it tends to invite people to put more of themselves into their work. People want to know that what they are doing is making a difference and helping their company.

And the number one motivator is involvement in decision making. That is what is sometimes called empowerment, giving them permission to make decisions that effect their own work lives. "

Maury said, "I thought you were going to say give them a raise, give them bonuses, have a party, pass out prizes and stuff like that."

Noah answered, "You can use those kinds of things to help emphasize what you are doing to motivate the people but used alone they are just band-aids. They are short term motivators that soon lose their effectiveness."

Maury said, "What do you suggest I do?"

"I suggest that you bring your team together and ask them to help you set the new higher goals. You could use an assessment tool like a personality profile to determine the kinds of motivators that work best with each individual person. And it doesn't hurt to ask them. They know more about their capabilities than you do and they need to be involved."

Noah was on a roll, "You can get a lot more out of your people if they feel like they will be recognized, if they are valued, if they believe that they are making a significant contribution to company profitability.

"Remember, people tend to support what they help to create. Then use the other techniques, parties and financial rewards to celebrate the gains you have made and recognize people for their accomplishments."

Maury was already working on the next meeting with his team in his mind. Then he remembered about the bathtub. "Noah, I'll call a couple of friends and we can take that tub down to the basement."

After they had pulled, lifted and hauled the antique tub into Maury's basement, Maury said to Noah, "I have another question to ask. Would you have time to coach me again next Saturday?"

"Sure," said Noah, "How about one o'clock?"

"I'm looking forward to it." said Maury as Noah climbed into his old truck.

During the week Maury noticed how well the concept of people supporting what they help to create fit in with the magic motivators. It was on Wednesday morning that he really got it.

Maury had done his daily planning of the work, was getting ready to assign the tasks when he heard himself ask, "Okay, team, here is the task ahead of us today." He was showing them his plan. "Now help me distribute the workload so that we get the best bang for our buck."

Red looked surprised. It took a minute before Maury realized that he had crossed a threshold of leadership. He was no longer just telling them what to do. He was actually depending on the combined intelligence and desire of his team to do it.

Red said where he thought he could make the best contribution. Linda did the same. Soon the whole team had worked out a way to get the work done.

Maury's shoulders felt lighter than they had since he started the team leader job. It was true that his people were willing to put more of themselves into their work when they were given respect, a challenge and an opportunity to have a say in how they did their work. It seemed that they had more energy. Good thing too. Because suddenly there was more work to do than ever. Soon he was flooded with an increase in business. It was a mixed blessing.

Chapter XI

The Value of Time

Maury wanted to talk with his team about a date to work on the new goals. But his plans were put on hold by some extra expedited orders and a breakdown on one of the packing machines and suddenly there wasn't time to work on the goal setting stuff.

By Saturday Maury was behind. He went in on his day off to catch up on paperwork. At a quarter after one he was just pulling into the yard when he remembered he had arranged to meet with Noah.

He rang Noah's door bell an waited while nothing happened. He wondered if Noah was gone when he heard the saw out in the garage.

"Hello, Noah," he said as he walked through the open garage door. "I'm sorry I'm late. I've been running around like a headless chicken all week."

Noah smiled and said, "And how about your bathroom project?"

Maury's face reddened, "I was hoping you wouldn't ask. The door to the bathroom is too small to get the tub in. The space in the bathroom is shaped wrong too. I have a lot of work to do."

Noah said, "Why don't we talk about planning ahead?"

Maury smiled, "Good idea. But I get so busy I don't have time to plan."

"I'm not surprised," said Noah, "but do you think you have any less time than anyone else?"

"No, of course not," Maury said. "But as a team leader I find my time all taken up with problems that come up every day. It seems the higher our productivity the less time I have to do anything but play catch up. I suppose it is unavoidable. It seems natural that when we are doing more it takes more time. I just wish I could work on something besides emergencies."

Noah pulled out his dry marker and used the side of the old refrigerator as he had before. He said, "Which of these do you think is the problem?" The white surface soon contained the following four statements: 'You don't have enough time available to do everything. You have too many things you are trying to do. You are spending too much time doing things. You are spending time on the wrong things.' "Which of these is really the problem?"

"Well," said Maury, "I think all of them apply in one way or another."

"What can we do about them?" asked Noah.

Maury took the marker and wrote responses to each of the statements. He read them aloud as he wrote, "The first thing I could do is, expand the time I spend on the things I need done. Second, I could reduce the things I try to do. Third, I could do things faster. And lastly, I could make better choices about the things I do."

"All these choices would help," said Noah. "The option you choose depends on your personal skills and the situation you wish to change. All options offer the potential to get more done."

Maury said, "This week it seemed like all my choices were made for me. I wish I could find a way to manipulate time."

"You've come to the right person," responded Noah. "After all, I am a time traveler."

"You said that before," Maury said with curiosity. "I was afraid you were some kind of a nut. I still don't know what you mean by that."

"We humans are natural time travelers," said Noah, his hand resting on the old refrigerator handle. "We generally travel forward in time, and at the regular rate, one day at a time. People don't think of it as time travel and don't think about the skill of navigating time as they progress toward the future. But I have made a study of the effects of time on our progress.

"There are some choices we can make in the present moment that will produce a big payoff in the future. People often treat their opportunities as if they are all alike. They don't realize that spending time is an investment. They don't realize how valuable time is and they spend it without thought."

"But what do you do when all of your time gets taken up by everything that is happening around. It feels like I don't have any choices about how I spend my time. I even had to go back in to work this morning because I didn't have enough time to get everything done during the week," said Maury.

Noah took a large piece of cardboard and laid it on the floor of the garage. He drew a large square and divided in four sections. Over the square he wrote the categories, 'present' and 'future.' On the left he labeled the sections, 'benefit' and 'loss.'

Maury watched Noah take an apple from the refrigerator and cut it up. He piled the seeds in the upper right section of the square, the apple slices in the upper left, the peelings in the lower left and from somewhere he produced a little green worm which he put in the lower right section.

"Maury," said Noah, "these are the four kinds of time investment. You invest your time and get something back from one of these categories, present benefits, future benefits, present losses or future losses. Can you think of activities that fit into the four categories?"

Maury stroked his chin with the forefinger and thumb of his right hand as he thought. He began slowly, "In the category of present benefit I put the activities of direct supervision such as coaching and controlling."

"What about when Red asks you a question to which he should already know the answer? Which category does that fall into?" Noah asked.

Maury surprised himself with his answer, "That depends on what I do about it. If I just answer the question, the time I spend fits into the category of apple peals. It is present loss. It is just like throwing my time in the trash."

Noah smiled and waited for Maury to continue.

He did, "But if I require him to answer the question himself and use the time to build his problem solving and decision making skills I am spending apple seed time. It is time which can be planted and expected to grow Red's productivity in the future."

Then with a new flash of insight Maury said, "And if I ignore the problem or make it worse by yelling at him it is worm time. I am creating growing problems and losses which will only get worse in the future. It is like a worm. It eats the value out of my future."

Noah clapped his hands together and said in a mock British accent, "Bravo. By George, I think you've got it. Do you have your planning calendar handy?"

Maury did. It was a small paperbacked calender that fit in his shirt pocket. He had picked it up at the drug store to keep appointments in case he had any.

Noah shook his head sadly and said, "Maury, you need to make an investment in your time storage device."

"You mean my calender?" asked Maury.

Noah spoke with seriousness, "Your time is too valuable to handle in such a haphazard way. You need to get a planning calender that has space for you to work on your future.

"When you divide up the future and make appointments and plans you need to identify where you should plant the seed time, where you want to spend the apple slice time, how to reduce the pealing time and eliminate the worm time.

"The only way you can secure the future is to go out into the white spaces in the future of your calender. Find calender space far enough in the future that it is not occupied with day-to-day appointments, and plan actions that will have payoffs.

"You need space to develop your ideas and keep track of your contacts and opportunities. Your own personal training and development plan should be there with the dates recorded on which you will make investments in yourself. You need to be able to anticipate the future and take action to shape it to your liking."

Maury could see that a little pocket calender might be enough for someone who didn't have much of a future. But he had bigger plans. He was going somewhere. He would definitely need a more detailed map of the road ahead.

When Maury left Noah's garage he felt like something had changed within him. With a little coaching he had reached way beyond what he would have alone. He felt proud.

He too was a time traveler, and not just a passenger; he was a driver. He was in charge of his future and on his way to success through professional growth.

He took charge of his basement project too. He opened up the back wall and expanded the floor space by two feet. Before he closed the wall up again he put the tub inside. It took a little remodeling and re-allocation of space and resources but he soon had his perfect bathroom complete.

About the Author

Bob Noah is president of Noah Onboard, a management consulting and training firm. He holds a master of management technology degree from University of Wisconsin-Stout. Bob's passion to understand people has taken him through postgraduate work in social work at the University of Iowa and many years of work in counseling and social work. Bob's undergraduate education is in religion and sociology. He conducts training workshops, coaches leaders, and helps companies go higher. Bob works with a wide variety of companies and organizations, always with an eye to improving the workplace, making it more effective and better for the people who work there.

To contact Noah Onboard:

Call toll free: (877)YES-NOAH
Email: bnoah@discover-net.net
Write: Noah Onboard
       E3164 County Road N, Boyceville
       Wisconsin, 54725

CPSIA information can be obtained at www.ICGtesting.com
Printed in the USA
LVOW042026110912

298392LV00002B/158/A